Previews of the Articles in this Volume

"Pursuant to the Confederate Congressional Act of October 13, 1862, the first Tennessee State Capitol notes were printed--and the irony begins."
--Mike Slate

"When an anthropologist from the University of Tennessee reconstructed the damage in Shy's skull, he found the wound too large to have been caused by a minie ball."
--Doris Boyce

"We have come to realize, however, that family history is much more than merely extracting a few facts from official records."
--Bonnie Ross Meador

"How many court buildings have stood on the public square in Nashville? Published sources offer conflicting information, some stating the number as four and others as five."
--Debie Cox

"Elm Hill Pike is one of the most historic roads in Nashville. Few thoroughfares in our city contain so much history packed into so few miles."
--Susan Douglas Wilson

"Jere Baxter attempted to acquire the right of way for his Tennessee Central. Frustrated by refusals to sell, he built new tracks nearly paralleling those of the NC&StL."
--Guy Alan Bockmon

"In February of 1851, after a successful campaign led by the local newspapers, P.T. Barnum was convinced to bring Jenny Lind, the Swedish Nightingale, to sing in the shiny new theater."
--Linda Center

"The monument's towering 50-foot granite shaft is actually seven years older than its year of dedication, and the story of the monument's creation in Nashville's first public park is nearly as interesting as the Robertson pioneers it memorializes."
--Ilene J. Cornwell

"All the big circus stars played Centennial Park: Clyde Beatty (whom I still consider the greatest of the lion and tiger trainers), the Wallendas of the high wire, the Zacchinis with their mammoth cannon, the Riding Hannefords, and the famous sad-faced clown Emmett Kelly."
--Dave Price

"With the proliferation of the family motor car in the 'Roaring Twenties,' excursions to the countryside became a popular pastime."
--Amelia Whitsitt Edwards

"From Rhoda Calvert Barnard, who has a planet for a namesake, to Cornelia Clark Fort, sacrificing her young life for her country, Nashville's daughters have lived with bravery and determination."
--Carol Kaplan

"For a great part of the 20th century Nashville residents either ignored or did not know that an area north of Jefferson Street was a prominent neighborhood where many of Nashville's leading citizens once lived."
--John Lawrence Connelly

"Kelley could not see why his son Robert had to commute across town to Pearl High School though the family lived within walking distance of East High School."
--James Summerville

"Four decades ago, during a time of sweeping social change throughout our nation, a determined group of Nashville students began a nonviolent revolution in this city that changed history."
--Sue Loper

"The building was constructed not only to store the State Library's growing collection, but also to preserve the state's archival records after many decades in which they were stuffed into attics, cellars, and odd corners of the Capitol and other buildings."
--Kathy Lauder

"The Archives' visitors--about 9,000 per year--have come from as near as Hillsboro High School and as far as Sophia, Bulgaria, to gain an understanding of the history of Nashville and how that history is preserved."
--Kenneth Fieth

"Memories can last a lifetime, and those with whom we experience special occasions live on, too."
--Houston Seat

"No language can paint the distress of many of the sufferers, who were left without bread, meat, dishes or plates, or a covering except the heavens."
--Submitted by Michael Ellis

"The Confederate Twenty-Dollar Irony"
and Other Essays from the
Nashville Historical Newsletter

Volume One in a Series

Compiled and edited by
Mike Slate and Kathy Lauder

Printed in the United States
by Classic Printing, Nashville, Tennessee

First Printing
October 2004

Design: Mike Slate
Index: Kathy Lauder

ISBN 0-9761680-0-6

Preface

Founded as a medium of historical sharing, the ***Nashville Historical Newsletter*** (***NHN***) published its first issue in January 1997. Before that time Nashville had no publication dedicated to saving and conveying the local historical knowledge of its citizens at large. From the beginning we invited all Nashvillians and others interested in our history to contribute short, previously unpublished essays and other material. The articles in this volume were selected from those originally appearing in various editions of the newsletter. Some of these essays have been revised slightly, and illustrations—some quite rare—have been added.

Our website (http://pages.prodigy.net/nhn.slate/), created in 1999, is a "bank" into which we continue to deposit bibliographies, essays, reminiscences, documents, and other articles. In November 2002 Kathy Lauder joined the staff, adding a dynamic dimension to all our efforts. The last hard copy of the *NHN* was published in December 2002, and the newsletter has continued in e-mail form only, publishing essay editions as well as news releases from area historical groups. We welcome new subscribers and contributors to our free online site. To join the list or to propose or submit an essay, write NHN.slate@prodigy.net.

This volume is the first of a series of such compilations. We have selected the entertaining and educational articles herein, along with their illustrations, in the hope of introducing newcomers to the pleasures of Nashville history, as well as providing longstanding Nashvillians with new episodes from their heritage.

The ***Nashville Historical Newsletter*** stresses historical accuracy but permits authors to decide whether to footnote their work with source information. If the reader discovers any errors of fact in this book, please contact us.

Mike Slate
October 2004

Foreword

Nearly 600,000 people reside in Nashville-Davidson County, Tennessee. If only one percent of them would research and write short essays on aspects of Nashville history, they would produce 6,000 articles! What an invaluable gift to the future that would be.

Such a heritage project seems utopian, hardly possible to achieve; yet with determination, organization, and cooperation it can be done. How can we start? Actually, we have already begun: authors have contributed more than 60 essays to the *Nashville Historical Newsletter*, including those in this book.

The *NHN* invites all Nashvillians—and all others interested in the history of our area—to submit brief articles to us (300 to 700 words). Essays should be e-mailed to NHN.slate@prodigy.net.

Together we can honor the past, inspire the present, and ensure the dignity of the future.

This illustration of the Tennessee State Capitol is from Edward King's book, *The Great South*, American Publishing Co., 1875. The church building in the left foreground, situated on Summer Street (today's Fifth Avenue), was the First Baptist Church from about 1841 to 1884. From that time until 1951 it served as the First Lutheran Church building.

<u>Acknowledgements</u>

This book, as well as much other work of the **Nashville Histori-cal Newsletter,** is possible because of the generosity of the contributors of essays and other articles. The writers have shared their work freely, expecting and receiving nothing in return. To them we—and all citizens of Nashville—owe a large debt of gratitude.

For several years we have depended on the expertise of Debie Cox of the Metro Archives. Debie has tolerated countless interruptions to her normal workload, checking facts and providing original information. To her we extend our heartfelt thanks.

Over time we have consulted with several other Nashville historians whose helpfulness has been inestimable. These include Jim Hoobler, James Summerville, Dave Price, Ilene Cornwell, Fletch Coke, Guy Bockmon, Amelia Edwards, Robbie Jones, and Peggy Dillard. We also thank Davidson County Historian John Connelly for his constant encouragement and for providing the message on the back of this book.

Of course, our work has often depended upon the efforts of previous historians, writers, and publishers. To all the trailblazers of Nashville history we owe great respect and tribute.

Also from King's book, a view of Nashville from the Capitol.

To one of Tennessee's fine families:

Tim, Leigh Ann, and Mary Leigh Slate

Table of Contents

Illustration Source Abbreviations

GL=Gary Layda, Metro Photographer
MANDC=Metropolitan Archives of Nashville & Davidson County
NHN=Nashville Historical Newsletter
NR=Nashville Room, Nashville Public Library
TSLA=Courtesy of Tennessee State Library and Archives
WNFM=West Nashville Founders' Museum

Circa 1909 postcard featuring the residential area just south of the Capitol. Today this area includes Legislative Plaza and the War Memorial Building. *-NHN-*

The Confederate Twenty-Dollar Irony

By Mike Slate

From 1862 through 1864 the Confederate States of America printed an estimated ten million twenty-dollar notes featuring an engraving of the Tennessee State Capitol. Today many of these notes survive in the hands of collectors and others, who may be unaware of the historical irony surrounding this currency.

Early Confederate twenty-dollar bills featured representations of a sailing vessel and various classical goddesses as well as a bust of CSA Vice President Alexander H. Stephens. Pursuant to the Confederate Congressional Act of October 13, 1862, the first Ten-

nessee State Capitol notes were printed--and the irony begins. This note's design shows miniscule yet visibly genteel folk apparently strolling the Capitol grounds. How-ever, months earlier, on February 25, 1862, Nash-ville Mayor R.B. Cheatham had surrendered the panicked city of Nash-

Vignette on Confederate $20 note -*NHN*-

ville to Union General Don Carlos Buell. Long before October 13 Confederate currency was worthless in Nashville.

With the Federal occupation of Nashville came the immediate securing of the statehouse and the hoisting of William Driver's famous flag, "Old Glory," on Capitol Hill. To be sure, no Southern-ers lolled around the Capitol grounds after February 25. Iron-fisted military governor Andrew Johnson arrived in Nashville on March 12. By the time of the October 13 Act, the Capitol was undergoing heavy fortification as Fort Andrew Johnson.

It seems likely that, although the "Tennessee Capitol" note was issued twice more (following the Act of March 23, 1863, and the Act of February 17, 1864), many Nashvillians did not see this cur-rency until years after its initial printing. The bill was engraved--and presumably printed--by the firm of Keatinge & Ball in Columbia, South Carolina, a city significantly distant from occupied Nashville. More of these notes may exist in Nashville today than at any time during the Civil War.

The Tennessee Capitol vignette was engraved probably by Edward Keatinge, who had worked for the American Bank Note Company in New York City. Recruited by the Confederacy for its treasury department, Keatinge teamed with Virginian Thomas A. Ball to form Keatinge & Ball in Richmond. Soon the firm removed to Columbia, South Carolina, a strategically safer location. There they produced Confederate currency using equipment and supplies smuggled from Europe through the Federal blockade. General Sherman destroyed the firm's facilities in February 1865.

Only two other Southern capitol buildings adorned Confederate currency: those of Columbia, South Carolina, and Richmond, Virginia. Despite the irony of its issuance, the Tennessee Capitol twenty-dollar bill is a tribute to an architectural gem, the timeless work of Philadelphia architect William Strickland.

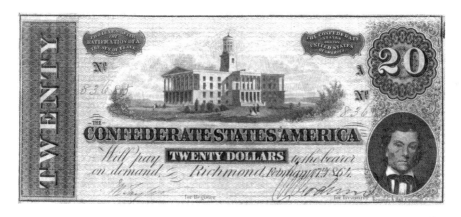

The Confederate "Tennessee Capitol" note included a bust of CSA Vice President Alexander H. Stephens. *-NHN-*

The Battle of Nashville:
Shy, Smith, & Hood

By Doris Boyce

A detail in the death of a Williamson County Civil War hero was clarified after Colonel William Shy's grave was desecrated in 1977. Until that time it was believed he had died from a minie ball shot from a muzzle-loading firearm on the second day of the Battle of Nashville, December 16, 1864. When an anthropologist from the University of Tennessee reconstructed the damage in Shy's skull, he found the wound too large to have been caused by a minie ball. Shy's injury was more likely inflicted by shrapnel from the heavy Union bombardment that Nashville citizens had watched from the distant Capitol Hill.

William Mabry Shy, Colonel of the 20th Tennessee, was left dead on the top of what was then Compton Hill. When his body was recovered, it had been stripped naked and bayoneted to a tree. The family still has the bayonet. General Benton Smith, Shy's superior officer, had been given specific orders by Hood to hold Compton Hill, "regardless of what transpires around you." Smith was taken prisoner at the bottom of the hill and beaten over the head three or four times with a saber. He never recovered, and his life ended in an insane asylum.

General John Bell Hood, Confederate commander of the battle, seemed to associate valor with casualties. Hood was a none-too-stable combat veteran who had to be tied on his horse because of a useless arm and an amputated leg. Sixteen days earlier, on November 30th, Hood had attacked the Union Army in the bloody one-day Battle of Franklin, which resulted in some 7,000 Confederate casualties.

The Battle of Nashville thrust 21,000 of Hood's poorly supplied infantry and 4,000 cavalry against General George H. Thomas's well-equipped Union infantry, about 60,000 strong. The fighting took place in the hills around present-day Harding Place/Battery Lane and spread over five miles, from Franklin Road to Hillsboro Pike. The Union bombarded the Southern lines for two days before charging with overwhelming force. Confederate survivors limped away as best they could via Hillsboro and Granny White pikes. According to the *Nashville Daily Press*, the two days of fighting resulted in 4,000 Union and 3,000 Confederates killed or wounded, as well as 3,000 Confederates captured.

After the Battle of Nashville, Hood, a West Point graduate who believed in frontal attacks with flags flying, retreated to Mississippi. In January of 1865, less than one month later, he gave up command, having all but destroyed the Army of Tennessee. Hood died in relative obscurity after ten years as a successful New Orleans businessman.

The valor of the Confederate dead will not be forgotten, since a few names have been honored, representing the many who died. In 1968 the Metro Historical Commission placed a plaque at the slope of Compton Hill, which had been re-named Shy's Hill. The site can be accessed by Shy's Hill Road or by Benton Smith Road from Harding Place, two blocks west of Granny White Pike.

Created by sculptor Giuseppe Moretti, the Battle of Nashville Peace Monument was erected in 1927. Its bronze horses represent the North and the South, whose Civil War armies engaged in the Battle of Nashville on December 15-16, 1864. The youth, by yoking the horses together, commemorates a united America during World War I. The original monument was prominently located on Franklin Pike. In 1999 the refurbished monument, pictured here, was rededicated in its own small park at Battlefield Drive and Granny White Pike, not far from its original site.

-NHN-

The Quest for Joshua Burnett Ross

By Bonnie Ross Meador

Joshua Burnett Ross, named for his maternal grandfather, was born in Jackson Township, Clermont County, Ohio, in 1842. He was the first of eleven children born to Osmore L. and Jerusha Loveland Burnett Ross, who had been married in Jackson Township on April 14, 1839.

In the 1850s Osmore Ross moved his family to Clark County, Illinois, where he had purchased farm acreage at auction for $200. (Total interest on the mortgage was $20.) The Rosses lived on the outskirts of Casey and Crooked Creek, not far from Hazel Dell. According to the 1860 Illinois census, Joshua Ross, then 17, was a chair maker.

We have come to realize, however, that family history is much more than merely extracting a few facts from official records. Our passion for it grew out of reading *The Red Badge of Courage* as children and wanting to make a connection to our past through the War Between the States. It was this hope that led us on our quest.

The bits and pieces collected through family anecdotes, newspaper stories, and photographs were elusive to trace, since the family has roots in Massachusetts, New Jersey, New York, Ohio, Kentucky, Tennessee, Oklahoma, Minnesota, Utah, Oregon, California, Washington, North Carolina, and Texas. We could find nothing on Joshua beyond the 1860 census. Then I remembered *The Red Badge of Courage*, and a new adventure unfolded. With notebook, camera, and filing cabinet in tow, we traveled to Clark County, Illinois, to get a more authentic feeling for the family by visiting the old homestead, walking in their footsteps, and touching their gravestones. But there was still no Joshua . . ..

With the help of a librarian from Greenup, Illinois, and after days of Internet research, Joshua began to emerge from the shadows. Records showed that the young chair maker had joined the Federals and become a Union soldier: on June 28, 1861, he mustered into the 21st Illinois Infantry, Company H, in Mattoon, Illinois, a few miles from his home.

Joshua's first commanding officer was Colonel Ulysses S. Grant, who was replaced by Colonel John W. S. Alexander when Grant received his promotion from the President. The 21st fought valiantly at Perryville, Kentucky, and at Stones River, near Murfreesboro, Tennessee, where the regiment was assigned to General Rosecrans. We were amazed to find that on their march to Stones River, the 21st had camped on Dumont Hill in Scottsville, Kentucky, the town where we presently reside.

The National Archives forwarded the information that Joshua had been wounded in the upper left chest area during the Battle of Stones River, December 1862. He was transferred to U.S. General Hospital #19, in the Morris and Stratton Building on Market Street-- now 2nd Avenue--in Nashville, where he died of his injuries on February 22, 1863. Joshua Burnett Ross was buried in grave 3634 in a temporary cemetery located near the hospital. His remains were later moved to Section E, Grave 0730, in the Nashville National Cemetery.

Jerusha Ross filed for her son's pension on June 30, 1880, seventeen and one-half years after his death. Joshua's brother, Silas L. Ross, named one of his sons after him: that child, Joshua Burnett Ross, was my grandfather.

Grave marker of Joshua B. Ross in Nashville National Cemetery.
-Meador-

Engraved on a brass plate near the arched marble gateway of the National Cemetery are the words of Abraham Lincoln's "Gettysburg Address," a fitting tribute to my great-great-uncle and all who lie beside him. On July 4, 2004, a hot Sunday afternoon, armed with advice from the *Nashville Historical Newsletter* and its readers, we were able to walk directly to Joshua's grave. Knowing he was from a poor farm family who lived far away, we had little doubt that we were the first family members to stand at his gravesite. Our visit to the National Cemetery, the close of a great adventure, brought us a step closer to knowing where we came from. Our lives are made richer by the knowledge that my great-great-uncle gave his life for us and for the hope of an America undivided.

Contemporary photo of the gateway of the Nashville National Cemetery on Gallatin Road. The pediment reads: "National Military Cemetery. Nashville A. D. 1867."
-Meador-

Old postcard, postmarked in 1908, featuring the gateway of the Nashville National Cemetery.
-NHN-

Courthouses of Davidson County, Tennessee

By Debie Cox

How many court buildings have stood on the public square in Nashville? Published sources offer conflicting information, some stating the number as four and others as five. Research in the minute books of the Davidson County Court has provided the following details.

First Courthouse

The building of the first Courthouse was authorized by the Davidson County Court at the October Term 1783: "The Court then proceeded to fix on a place for Building of a Courthouse & Prison, and agree that in the present situation of the Settlement that it be at Nashborough and Built at the Expense of the Publick. And that the size of the Courthouse be eighteen feet square in the body with a Leanto Shade of twelve feet on the one side of the length of the House. And that the house be furnished with the necessary benches, Barr, Table &c fit for the Reception of the Court." In April of 1792 the Court "ordered that David Hay repair the Court house by Making Two Doors well fixed and Hung with three window shutters well hung; and the house Well chinked."

Second Courthouse

Davidson County Court minutes of October 15, 1802, page 367, report as follows: "Court adjourns for five minutes, to meet in the new Courthouse. Court met according to adjournment in the New Courthouse where was present...." A further search of Court minutes yields few clues as to the size or type of building. In 1804 the Court ordered the purchasing of a bell for the Courthouse and in 1806 the painting of the roof and steps. In 1822 the Court "ordered that opening at the head of the Stairs be closed, leaving a door there to which he shall have a shutter made and to have the two stoves placed one on each side of the house behind the bar with pipes extending so as to render the house comfortable for the different courts that are to set here during the winter...." In October 1825 a commission was appointed to determine whether the Courthouse could be repaired to make it comfortable enough for the Court to meet in winter or whether it would be necessary to rent a building for the winter.

Third Courthouse

In January 1826 the acting Justices of the Court met and voted to raise, with a special tax, $15,000 over a period of three years for the purpose of building a courthouse for the county. The Courthouse was finished in late 1829 or early 1830. It is described in Eastin Morris's *Tennessee Gazetteer*, 1834: "The Court House which stands on the public square, is a spacious and commodious edifice. It presents a handsome front of 105 feet and is sixty-three feet deep. The basement story contains a number of rooms, designed for public offices, and on the second and third floors there are two rooms forty by sixty feet each, two others thirty-six by forty, and two others twenty-three by forty. The basement story is eleven feet high, and the two principal ones are eighteen feet each, and the height of the whole building to the top of the dome is ninety feet. The foundation and part of the lower story is of fine hewn stone, and the remainder of brick, and the two fronts are ornamented with four white pilasters each. The dome contains a good town clock, and is supported by eight columns of Ionic order." This Courthouse burned in 1856. The County Court minutes state: "Monday Morning April 14, 1856 Court met pursuant to adjournment at the State House in Nashville (the Court House having been burned down)."

Fourth Courthouse

On May 10, 1856, the Court met in the Market House: "The County Court will build a Courthouse on or near the center of the Public Square in Nashville." According to County Court minutes, architect W. Francis Strickland, son of William Strickland, designer of the Tennessee State Capitol, was "employed at a salary of one thousand dollars per annum as architect of the court house." The design chosen by Strickland was very similar to that of the Capitol building designed by his father. The building was to have a basement and three stories above ground, and was to be 118 feet by 72 feet in size. The Court first met in the new building in January 1859. The building was remodeled in 1910 with an additional story added. In 1935 this building, along with the City Hall and Market House, was demolished to make room for a new courthouse.

Fifth Courthouse

The present Courthouse was completed in 1937. The architects, Emmons H. Woolwine of Nashville and Frederic C. Hirons of New York, won an architectural competition in 1935 with their Art Deco design. The cornerstone of the building was laid August 10, 1936, and the building was dedicated on December 8, 1937. The general contractor was J. A. Jones Construction Company. The building is eight stories high and measures 260 feet by 96 feet. The years have taken a toll: the building is in need of repair, and the need for space is critical. Mayor Bill Purcell hopes to relieve the crowded conditions in the Courthouse by the construction of a General Sessions-Criminal Court complex, near the Ben West building. A major renovation of the Courthouse is currently underway.

Construction of the third courthouse was completed near the end of 1829. The building was destroyed by fire on April 13, 1856.
-MANDC-

Francis Strickland, son of William Strickland, was the architect for the fourth courthouse, first occupied in December of 1858. The design chosen by the younger Strickland was similar to the Capitol building designed by his father. *-NHN-*

The cornerstone of the fifth courthouse was laid August 10, 1936, and the building was dedicated on December 8, 1937. -MANDC-

Touring Elm Hill Pike

By Susan Douglas Wilson

Elm Hill Pike is one of the most historic roads in Nashville. Few thoroughfares in our city contain so much history packed into so few miles. The road, which probably began as a buffalo or Indian trail, has been mentioned in several accounts of early Nashville history. Andrew Jackson was reported to be a frequent traveler on Elm Hill Pike on his journeys from downtown Nashville to the Hermitage. Mapmakers and old-timers have also referred to this road as "Chicken Pike."

Mt. Ararat Cemetery gate. *-NHN-*

As you turn off of Murfreesboro Pike onto Elm Hill Pike, the first historic site encountered is Mt. Ararat Cemetery on the north. Mount Ararat was founded in 1869 by local black leaders and became a burial ground for many of Nashville's black pioneers. Over the years, the cemetery became a dumping ground and a target for vandals. In 1982 the management of Mt. Ararat was taken over by the Greenwood Cemetery's board of directors, who voted to change the name from Mt. Ararat to Greenwood Cemetery West and to begin a comprehensive restoration project.

About a mile east of Mt. Ararat Cemetery is Greenwood Cemetery, established on thirty-seven acres in 1888 by Preston Taylor. Taylor, born a slave in Louisiana in 1849, was an influential black preacher, undertaker, and business leader. In addition to Taylor, illustrious Nashville citizens buried at Greenwood Cemetery include Z. Alexander Looby, the Rev. Kelly Miller Smith, Sr., DeFord Bailey, John Merritt, and J. C. Napier.

In 1906 Preston Taylor opened Greenwood Park on approximately forty acres adjoining Greenwood Cemetery. The park was established to serve the black community and included a baseball stadium, skating rink, swimming pool, theater, merry-go-round, bandstand, zoo, and many other attractions. A state-wide fair and a Boy Scout summer camp were also held at Greenwood Park. The admission to the park was ten cents on regular days and twenty-five cents on holidays. The Fairfield-Green streetcar stop was nearby, and horse-drawn wagons would pick up patrons and deliver them to the park's entrance at Lebanon Road and Spence Lane. Preston Taylor died in 1931, and his wife managed the park until its closing in 1949.

Preston Taylor's gravestone in Greenwood Cemetery. *-NHN-*

Buchanan's Station was located about another mile east where Mill Creek crosses Elm Hill Pike. The station was established by John Buchanan in 1780. Twelve years later an oft-recounted Indian battle ensued. On a moonlit night in 1792 a band of three hundred Creek and Cherokee, under the leadership of Chiachattalla, raided the station. The twenty-one settlers fought bravely and defeated their attackers, killing Chiachattalla. Major Buchanan lived at the station until his death in 1832. He is buried, along with his wife and other settlers, in the station's cemetery.

Peabody College established the Seaman A. Knapp School of Rural Life in 1915 on one hundred fifty acres on Elm Hill Pike. More acreage, including the site of Buchanan's Station, was acquired in 1922. The farm was the first institution in the United States devoted to the study of the problems of rural life. Peabody College officials believed that teachers should become acquainted with agricultural life since so many of them would be teaching in rural areas. The experimental farm became a showplace, with award-winning dairy and beef cattle herds. Innovative techniques in irrigation, pasturage, and field equipment were tested at the farm; and many crops were raised, including a certified corn station and a contoured, twenty-five acre orchard. Knapp Farm provided Peabody

College with all its meat, vegetables, and fruit until World War II. The importance of the farm declined after the 1920s because of state-supported agricultural research. Expensive to maintain, Knapp Farm was sold in 1965 to a contractor who developed it into an industrial park.

Though the exact location of Mud Tavern is disputed, most old-timers agree that it was near the intersection of Elm Hill Pike and McGavock Pike. The tavern, built during Nashville's youth, was made of cedar logs with a mud and stick chimney. Andrew Jackson was a frequent patron, and it is reported that he spent two days there planning strategy in his duel with the ill-fated Charles Dickinson. Years later a community named Mud Tavern grew up in the area and included a railroad station, school, post office, and grocery store. The Mud Tavern school building was used for many years as a clubhouse by the Elm Hill Community Club.

The Buchanan Log House. *-NHN-*

On the far side of Donelson Pike, at the corner of Elm Hill Pike and Hurt Drive, is the James Buchanan house. This two-story log house was built *circa* 1809. James Buchanan and his wife are buried in the family graveyard near the house, which is now under the care of the Association for the Preservation of Tennessee Antiquities.

At the present time, Elm Hill Pike ends at Bell Road. The east-ern-most part of the road has been re-engineered several times. The course of the road itself may change, but the history of Elm Hill Pike will always remain as a significant part of Nashville's heritage.

Ghostly Tracks of the Tennessee and Pacific Railroad

By Guy Alan Bockmon

According to Elmer G. Sulzer's fascinating book, *Ghost Railroads of Tennessee*, the grandiosely titled Tennessee and Pacific Railroad Company was chartered in 1867. It was to connect Knoxville and Jackson, Mississippi, via Nashville and Memphis.

By 1877 the T&P was serving Nashville, Mt. Olivet, Mud Tavern, Donelson, Hermitage, Green Hill, Mt. Juliet, Silver Springs, Leeville (Stringtown), Tucker's Gap, and Lebanon. By 1888 the system had become a branch of the NC&StL.

Jere Baxter attempted to acquire the right of way for his Tennessee Central. Frustrated by refusals to sell, he built new tracks nearly paralleling those of the NC&StL. Excursion trains operated by the Tennessee Central Museum still use the TC tracks. The last train ran on the T&P tracks in 1935.

South and west of Elm Hill Pike at Mill Creek I found few remains of the T&P; but visible from both Elm Hill Pike and Massman Drive an abandoned railroad bridge is burdened with junked rail cars. Eastward from there the former roadbed is marked by rows of power lines marching through the industrial area and across Acorn, Wanda, and Sanborn Drives and then across Briley Parkway.

On the south side of Elm Hill Pike, east of Ermac Drive, stone support walls of the railroad bridge which once crossed Sims Branch still exist. The right-of-way reappears on the west side of McGavock Pike, north of Elm Hill Pike. The two-mile grade from Mud Tavern to Donelson Pike climbed about 100 feet. The N.E.S. poles are visible from Lakeland Drive a few yards above the Gateway Missionary Baptist Church and, farther east, from Seneca Drive.

The old railroad bed near Lakeland Drive. *-NHN-*

West of the intersection of McCampbell Road and Donelson Pike a driveway occupies the roadbed. Nearby Donelson Station changed the name of the former McWhirtersville.

Eastward from Donelson Pike, McCampbell Road runs on the right of and parallel with the procession of power poles. Before crossing Stewart's Ferry Pike the pair of roadbeds begin a parallel course.

At the N.E.S. substation on Stewart's Ferry Pike the power lines terminate. TSLA's "Davidson County, ca. 1920, Map #1009" (selected portion below, used by permission) shows that the two roadbeds diverged between Stones River and Central Pike. The T&P roadbed then became Chandler Road from Central Pike east. At Old Lebanon Dirt Road TC track and T&P roadbed resume their side-by-side positions.

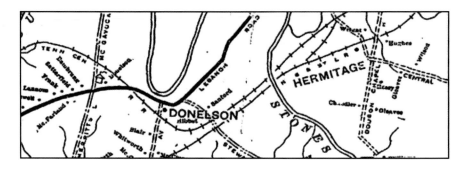

After crossing Tulip Grove Road, Chandler Road is renamed West Division and, beyond Mt. Juliet, East Division. The twin roadbeds continue into Rutland, where the tracks veer to the north. At Highway 109, the road doglegs right and left. Renamed Leeville Pike, it continues into Lebanon.

To see a representation of the end-of-the-line, turn-around wye go to http://MapsOnUs.switchboard.com, call up a map of Lebanon, TN, center on "Tennessee Blvd" at "S Cumberland Av," and "zoom in."

Chancery Court, the Adelphi, and Adolphus Heiman

By Linda Center

The Davidson County Chancery Court dockets located at Metro Archives are a little-known and greatly under-utilized resource for Nashville history. Established in 1836, Chancery Court for this district was held in Franklin, Williamson County, until 1846. In that year a separate court was formed for Davidson County, with Terry H. Cahal appointed as Chancellor. With the goal of cleaning, flattening, and indexing dockets dating from 1846 through 1875, volunteers and staff at the Archives have completed the years through the Civil War. From over 4,300 dockets a database of over 45,000 entries has been created, which includes the names of principals, family members, and slaves.

The dockets from these early cases, some of which continued for years, contain a wealth of details about daily life in Nashville and Middle Tennessee. The depositions, exhibits, and supporting papers are lively documents describing personal items of dress, toiletries, medicines, and sometimes personal appearance. When reading the depositions, which were phonetically recorded by the clerk, the speech patterns, pronunciations, and idioms of the day come through loud and clear. Some documents contain vivid descriptions of people, places, and buildings long gone. Consider the case of *Gilman et al. v. The Adelphi Theatre Company*, filed April 23, 1851.

In 1850 the Adelphi company was incorporated by the state and proceeded to purchase property on North Cherry Street (4th Avenue). The major stockholders in the company were Anthony Vanleer, J. Walker Percy, and Hugh Kirkman. The company hired Adolphus Heiman to design a "costly and handsome edifice suitable for theatrical performances." Timothy W. Gilman, of Gilman & Hughes, submitted his bid of $8,000 and $200 in stock in the company and was selected as chief carpenter and mechanic under Heiman's supervision. Maj. Heiman's design, completed at a cost of

Adolphus Heiman's signature.
-MANDC-

$25,000, was indeed handsome, with a two-story arched entrance which led to the brick-paved lobby. A ventilation system and other up-to-the-minute features were prominent in the plan. The theatre reputedly had the second largest stage in America at the time.

Gilman found Heiman's supervision arbitrary and his plans "so vague and indefinite as scarcely to form a basis for a contract and so frequently and repeatedly were they departed from when they were specific that they furnish scarcely a shadow of the work after it was completed." In several instances, states Gilman, "when the work had been done according to the original design said Heiman would change his plan have it pulled down taken away and something different put in its stead."

Opening night, July 1, 1850, was a gala affair. The opening notice ran in the *Republican Banner* immediately following the Sexton's report of burials in the city cemetery—five of the seven deaths were from cholera. "The Theatre- Opens to-night...and we expect to see a large audience on hand...to see the interior of one of the prettiest and best establishments of the kind in the West or South." Although, as the notice stated, it was not considered "an auspicious time to commence operations," Nashville's finest did indeed turn out for the premier performance. The epidemic struck with a vengeance that week. The *Banner* called for limited or no July 4th celebrations and did not publish on July 5th, but the Adelphi opened every night of its first week.

In February of 1851, after a successful campaign led by the local newspapers, P.T. Barnum was convinced to bring Jenny Lind, the Swedish Nightingale, to sing in the shiny new theater. However, a third tier of box seats was deemed necessary to accommodate the anticipated crowds, and William Strickland was hired to design the added tier. Gilman & Hughes were once again chief carpenters. They agreed and bound themselves "to make the alterations and enlargements of the interior of the Adelphi Theatre according to the plan now furnished by ( ) Strickland as Architect...to be finished so it can be used comfortably on the night of the 31(st) March present, being the time fixed as the first concert to be given by Jenny Lind...." Gilman & Hughes charged $1,500 for their services: $1,000 from P.T. Barnum, $250 from the Adelphi Theatre Company, and $250 from ticket subscriptions from hotels and other businesses.

The company did not pay its debts in a timely fashion, and in April of 1851, Heiman, Gilman, Strickland, and the other contractors sued. The depositions and bills give a vivid picture of the construction and finishing touches to the building. The court clerk's copy of Heiman's written "plan and specifications" describes "a ground story of 142 feet by 65 feet front on Cherry Street...with a room on each side of the main entrance of 19 by 23 feet, to be furnished with doors and side lights. All the doors of exit and entrance, are to be put upon pivots instead of hinges, so that they may be opened and shut in either way by any pressure from within or without." All flooring, seats, doors, box fronts, and the roof shingles were "to be made of well seasoned poplar." The stage was furnished with four traps and two stairways leading to the rear of the stage from below.

The leading businesses in Nashville had claims against the theater company. A.G. Payne supplied the stone for the two-foot-thick foundation and completed the masonry work. Samuel Watkins completed the brickwork for $3,437.89. Painters Hutcherson & Flemming used paints purchased from Kirkman & Ellis Hardware— and what colors: sienna, yellow ochre, rose pink, Vandyke brown, Paris green, Prussian blue, Venetian red, chrome yellow, red, and green. From McNairy & Hamilton came books of gold leaf and gallons of lead and turpentine. Claiborne & Macey supplied braces, pulleys, plates, chains, hooks, and brackets. From W. & R. Freeman came gilt frames, yards of damask and gimp, silk tassels, a pair of "curtain ornaments," and 689 feet of gilt molding.

Chancellor A.O.P. Nicholson decreed that the theater should be sold at public auction to pay all debts against the company. Heiman, acting as agent for the creditors, offered the winning bid of $10,000. The property was to be "vested in them as tennants [*sic*] in common," the share of each creditor to be in proportion to his claim against the company. Heiman failed to "execute his notes," the theatre was again put up for sale, and W.W. Wetmore made the winning bid. The creditors were paid at last. William Strickland, as a

Class III claimant, was paid after all other debts were satisfied. He received $100 for his services.

In the 1870s the ownership changed again, and the Adelphi became the Grand Opera House. The theater was gutted by fire in 1902, but the façade with its arched entry remained standing. The theater was rebuilt and reopened in 1904 as the Bijou. Other theaters and businesses on Church Street were drawing the crowds away from Fourth Avenue, and the Bijou closed in 1913. It was rescued again in 1916 when the Bijou Amusement Company reopened the doors as the Bijou Theater for Negroes. The Bijou was one of a chain of theaters throughout the south.

The Bijou was a venue for movies, vaudeville shows, concerts, and boxing matches. Ethel Waters, Bessie Smith, and Ma Rainey entertained packed houses. Special nights were set aside for white audiences to hear blues greats like Smith and her sister Mamie with the band, the Jazz Hounds. The tornado of 1933 lifted the roof and dropped part of it across the street. However, not a performance was missed, and, under a temporary roof, the Bijou was open again the next day.

The Adelphi-Grand-Bijou Theater stood at 423 4th Avenue North for over one hundred years through bankruptcy, fire, and storms. In 1957 it fell to the wrecking ball to make way for the new Municipal Auditorium.

Old postcard of the Bijou Theater, *circa* 1910.
-NHN-

The Robertson Monument: From Exposition Capstone to Centennial Park Monolith

By Ilene J. Cornwell

April 24, 2004, marked the 224th anniversary of the historical founding of Nashville. On that well-known date in 1780, John Donelson's flotilla of about 30 flatboats and several pirogues completed the 1006-mile voyage via four rivers to the French Lick's almost-completed log central station. Here the travelers joined James Robertson's overland settlement party that had traveled into the western North Carolina frontier to cross the frozen Cumberland River on Christmas Day, 1779, to establish an outpost of civilization. This two-prong settlement of Nashville was described by Theodore Roosevelt in *Winning of the West* as "being equal in importance to the settlement of Jamestown or the landing at Plymouth Rock."

Not as well known is we recently passed the 100th anniversary of the October 11, 1903, dedication of the Robertson Monument in Centennial Park. The monument's towering 50-foot granite shaft is actually seven years older than its year of dedication, and the story of the monument's creation in Nashville's first public park is nearly as interesting as the Robertson pioneers it memorializes.

The monument's existence is due to the energy, dedication, and vision of Nashville's Major Eugene C. Lewis (1845-1917), owner of the *Nashville American* newspaper and a consulting civil engineer. It was Lewis's friend, local architect William C. Smith, who suggested in a late-1893 speech to Nashville's Commercial Club that "a spectacular Tennessee Centennial be held to alleviate financial distress and to divert the attention of the people" from the long and severe depression that had engulfed America after the Panic of '93. Before the depression, according to W. F. Creighton in *Building of Nashville*, local attorney Douglas Anderson had suggested in local newspapers that a celebration be held in Nashville to commemorate the centenary of Tennessee's 1796 statehood. Although Anderson's earlier suggestion had evoked favorable public response, no action was taken until Smith renewed interest in the project. The Nashville Tennessee Centennial Exposition Company was formed and by the summer of 1895 was beginning to acquire financial support for the event. John W. Thomas, president of the Nashville, Chattanooga and St. Louis Railroad, served as president of the Centennial Company and chairman of the executive committee of the Exposition, and Major E. C. Lewis was named director general. The site selected for the Exposition was the West Side Race Track and Park, located on the old fairgrounds surrounding the historic Cockrill Springs area at the end of Church Street and the terminus of the West End Avenue streetcar line. The first Tennessee State Fair had been staged on the site in 1869, with subsequent fairs held in 1873, 1879, and 1884.

The Centennial Exposition, held May 1 through October 30, 1897, was "essentially a fair on a grand scale," wrote A. W. Crouch and H. D. Claybrook in *Our Ancestors Were Engineers*. Attractions included 12 large buildings featuring exhibits on the commercial, industrial, agricultural, and educational interests of the state; a "midway" including Egyptian, Cuban, and Chinese villages; a "Giant See-saw" designed by local engineer and steel fabricator Arthur J. Dyer; Venetian gondoliers on newly created Lake Watauga; a Venetian Rialto bridge designed by local architect C. A. Asmus; parades and "sham battles" by the Tennessee Militia; fireworks and other entertainment; and a 250-foot flagstaff designed by E. C. Lewis. Major Lewis had also conceived the idea to create a replica of the 5th-century B. C. Athenian Parthenon to house the art exhibit, and commissioned local architect W. C. Smith to make the needed drawings. (The Parthenon, built during 1895-1897, and the city park board's 1920 decision to have it rebuilt as a permanent structure is a story unto itself.)

Among the exhibits featured at the Exposition's Mineral and Forestry Building was a towering, 50-foot granite shaft. The impressive monolith is attributed to the "Barry Vermont Granite Quarries" by Creighton in *Building of Nashville*, but Leland Johnson wrote in *The Parks of Nashville* that the "granite shaft was quarried at Stone Mountain, Georgia, by Venerable [*sic*] Brothers of Atlanta and shipped to Nashville for display during the 1897 Centennial Exposition. Oral tradition says a portion of the shaft broke off during transit to Nashville." The shaft's original flat stone base remains today on the west bank of Lake Watauga and bears a metal plate commemorating the Centennial Exposition.

After the Exposition closed, all buildings except the Parthenon were torn down and removed. The success of the Exposition, as well as the progressive movement of the late 19th Century to establish public parks, planted the seed for Nashville's park system. In 1901 Mayor James Head appointed five men, one of whom was Major E. C. Lewis, to the new Board of Park Commissioners. Negotiations were begun by the city in early 1902 with the owners of the 72-acre Centennial Park to purchase the land for a permanent city park. After months of complicated offers and counter-offers, described in *The Parks of Nashville*, Nashville Railway and Light Company purchased Centennial Park, and its title was presented to the city park board on December 22, 1902.

On January 13, 1903, Major Lewis addressed the Tennessee Historical Society on the subject of James Robertson. He began his speech by informing the assembled members of "a fortunate circumstance that transpired only a few days ago. . . .For the first time in all its history, Nashville has park ground worthy of the Capital of Tennessee. The title to the Centennial Grounds, upon which the city has already contributed a large sum of money toward the adornment thereof, is now in the city of Nashville. The Park Commission. . .has so far determined upon but one measure, and that, the erection in Centennial Park of a monument [for] James Robertson, the founder of Nashville." He concluded his lengthy profile of Robertson by asking, "What have we of Nashville done to honor this man's memory? Has even the memory of all the good Robertson did been interred with his bones? . . .Are we a grateful people?"

Major Lewis had made prescient provisions to answer his own questions. When negotiations to purchase the Centennial land began, he had purchased the 50-foot granite shaft for $200; then his fellow-commissioner Samuel A. Champion "resolved that it be erected in the park as a monument to the memory of James Robertson." Lewis also purchased the flat stone base for $10 in 1903 to remain beside Lake Watauga as a memorial to the Centennial Exposition. A new granite base was needed to support the heavy shaft after its relocation, but no record has yet been found of the base's creator or its procurement. Wherever the massive base originated, Johnson described the monument's creation in *The Parks of Nashville*: "With a tripod made of three large oak logs and block and tackle, Major Lewis raised the shaft into position and then constructed the foundation beneath it." The granite shaft and its base weigh a total of 52.5 tons. Text is inscribed on a plaque on each side of the monument:

North Side Text

JAMES ROBERTSON

BORN IN BRUNSWICK COUNTY, VIRGINIA, JUNE 28, 1742. MOVED TO NORTH CAROLINA IN 1750. CAME TO TENNESSEE IN 1769. SETTLED NASHVILLE IN 1780. DIED IN TENNESSEE SEPT. 1, 1814. REINTERRED IN THE CITY CEMETERY AT NASHVILLE, 1825 UNDER AUTHORITY OF THE TENNESSEE LEGISLATURE.

East Side Text

CHARLOTTE REEVES
WIFE OF JAMES ROBERTSON

BORN IN NORTH CAROLINA, JAN. 2, 1751. MARRIED TO JAMES ROBERTSON, 1768. DIED IN NASHVILLE, JUN. 11, 1843. BURIED IN THE CITY CEMETERY. MOTHER OF THE FIRST MALE CHILD BORN AT NASHVILLE. SHE PARTICIPATED IN THE DEEDS AND DANGERS OF HER ILLUSTRIOUS HUSBAND: WON HONORS OF HER OWN AND ALONG HIS PATH OF DESTINY CAST A LEADING LIGHT OF LOYALTY, INTELLIGENCE AND DEVOTION.

South Side Text

A WORTHY CITIZEN OF BOTH VIRGINIA AND NORTH CAROLINA. PIONEER, PATRIOT AND PATRIARCH IN TENNESSEE. DIPLOMAT, INDIAN FIGHTER, MAKER OF MEMORABLE HISTORY. DIRECTOR OF THE MOVEMENT OF THE SETTLERS REQUIRING THAT HAZARDOUS AND HEROIC JOURNEY SO SUCCESSFULLY ACHIEVED FROM WATAUGA TO THE CUMBERLAND. FOUNDER OF NASH-

VILLE. BRIGADIER-GENERAL OF THE UNITED STATES ARMY.
AGENT OF THE GOVERNMENT TO THE CHICKASAW NATION. HE
WAS ERNEST, TACITURN, SELF-CONTAINED, AND HAD THAT
QUIET CONSCIOUSNESS OF POWER USUALLY SEEN IN BORN
LEADERS OF MEN. "HE HAD WINNING WAYS AND MADE NO FUSS."
(OCONNOSTOTA) HE HAD WHAT WAS OF VALUE BEYOND PRICE--
A LOVE OF VIRTUE, AN INTREPID SOUL, AN EMULOUS DESIRE
FOR HONEST FAME. HE POSSESSED TO AN EMINENT DEGREE THE
CONFIDENCE, ESTEEM AND VENERATION OF ALL HIS CONTEM-
PORARIES. HIS WORTH AND SERVICES IN PEACE AND WAR ARE
GRATEFULLY REMEMBERED. AMIABLE IN PRIVATE LIFE, WISE IN
COUNCIL, VIGILANT IN CAMP, COURAGEOUS IN BATTLE, STRONG
IN ADVERSITY, GENEROUS IN VICTORY, REVERED IN DEATH.

West Side Text

JAMES ROBERTSON
FOUNDER OF NASHVILLE

**"WE ARE THE ADVANCE GUARD OF CIVILIZATION. OUR WAY IS
ACROSS THE CONTINENT." ROBERTSON--1779**

The monument to James and Charlotte Reeves Robertson was presented to the city of Nashville on October 11, 1903, by Major E. C. Lewis on behalf of the Park Commission. About 100 Robertson descendants from all over the United States and one foreign country attended the ceremony in Centennial Park, according to Sarah F. Kelley in *Children of Nashville*. Three-year-old Dickson Wharton Robertson, descended through Dr. Peyton Robertson, was dressed in Scottish-plaid kilts and pulled the string to unveil the towering monument honoring his great-great-grandfather. Among those offering memorial tributes to Nashville's founder were Governor James B. Frazier and Mayor James Head.

"History often repeats itself," wrote Kelley. "On June 28, 1972, the descendants of James Robertson gathered once again in Nashville to celebrate Tennessee's 'James Robertson Day' proclaimed by Governor Winfield Dunn." Among the descendants gathered around the Robertson Monument in Centennial Park was the same Dickson Wharton Robertson who had participated in the monument's unveiling 69 years earlier.

As the Robertson Monument passes its centenary, the 108-year-old shaft has weathered well, as have the 101-year-old base and four bronze plaques. Attesting to the passage of a century is that the massive base appears to have sunk several feet into the earth since 1903. Without measured drawings to provide dimensions of the original base, however, a definitive conclusion cannot be made. Thus we celebrate the founding of Nashville with the hope that Centennial Park's terrain will continue to support the city's monument to its founder, so that future Nashvillians may enjoy a bicentennial celebration of the Robertson Monument.

Robertson Monument picture from *General James Robertson: Father of Tennessee*, by Thomas Edwin Matthews (Nashville: The Parthenon Press, 1934).
-WNFM-

SOURCES

Winning of the West, Volume II: From the Alleghenies to the Mississippi, 1777-1783, by Theodore Roosevelt (New York: G. P. Putnam's Sons, 1889).

Tennessee Old and New, Sesquicentennial Edition, 1796-1946, Volumes I and II (Nashville: Tennessee Historical Commission and Tennessee Historical Society, 1946).

Seedtime on the Cumberland, by Harriette Simpson Arnow (New York: The Macmillan Company, 1960).

Building of Nashville, by Wilbur Foster Creighton; revised and enlarged by Wilbur F. Creighton, Jr., and Leland R. Johnson (Nashville: Wilbur F. Creighton, Jr., and Elizabeth Creighton Schumann, 1969).

Children of Nashville: Lineages of James Robertson, by Sarah Foster Kelley (Nashville: Blue and Gray Press, 1973).

Our Ancestors Were Engineers, by Arthur Weir Crouch and Harry Dixon Claybrook (Nashville: Nashville Section of American Society of Civil Engineers, 1976).

The Parks of Nashville: A History of the Board of Parks and Recreation, by Leland R. Johnson (Nashville: Metropolitan Nashville and Davidson County Board of Parks and Recreation, 1986).

Andrew Jackson Slept Here: A Guide to Historical Markers in Nashville and Davidson County (Nashville: Metropolitan Historical Commission of Nashville and Davidson County, 1993).

World Wide Web URL for Tennessee State Fair
(http://www.tennesseestatefair.org/statefair.html)

The Centennial Circus Lot

By Dave Price

Back in the days when tent circuses traveled the land, there was a story told of an old showman being asked for his concept of the hereafter. He is said to have replied, "It must be like the circus lot in Nashville."

To the generation who grew up here prior to WWII, the Centennial Park athletic field on 25th Avenue (where the Sportsplex is now situated) was the city's principal circus lot. There a spacious, level, and grassy expanse welcomed the big tent circuses year after year.

The John Robinson Circus may have been the first to play this lot in 1910. Forepaugh-Sells Bros. was there in 1911. During the flamboyant years of the American circus, all the great railroad shows came to Centennial Park: Sells-Floto, Al G. Barnes, Hagenbeck-Wallace, and Cole Bros., to name a few. Barnum & Bailey and Ringling both played there prior to their unification in 1919; and the combined show then played the park most years through 1947, when the park board decided to close Centennial to circuses.

During that era, the flatcars would unload at Kayne Avenue, the

wagons being pulled up Division Street to the top of the hill and then over to West End. The zebras, camels, llamas, performing horses, and any elephants not needed for pulling wagons were unloaded from stock cars at the north end of the yards and led out Charlotte to 23rd Avenue, thence to the show grounds, going in the back way.

Circus elephants below Broad Street viaduct, *circa* 1940. -Price-

As you came on the lot from 25th, you would enter the "midway" area where the sideshow (with its congress of strange people) and numerous concession stands would be raised. Beyond that was the main entrance to the circus, which took you first into a long menagerie tent where you could walk cage to cage and from pen to corral viewing animals from the corners of the earth. I saw my first gorilla (the famous "Gargantua") here. The elephants might number from a dozen to forty, and it was not unusual to find giraffes, a rhino, and a hippo on display along with polar bears and other species not generally found in Nashville.

Working your way through the menagerie, you would find yourself in the big top, a mammoth canvas tent as long as a football field and seating several thousand. Here the actual circus performance took place, and it was always a good one. All the big circus stars played Centennial Park: Clyde Beatty (whom I still consider the greatest of the lion and tiger trainers), the

Circus tent and onlookers at Centennial Park. -Price-

Wallendas of the high wire, the Zacchinis with their mammoth cannon, the Riding Hannefords, and the famous sad-faced clown Emmett Kelly. Tom Mix was once here with Sells-Floto, and Jack Dempsey came with Cole Bros.

But those days are over; dead and gone. Apparently more dead than I'd realized. We recently overheard an old timer telling a member of a younger generation about the circuses he'd seen at Centennial Park. The listener responded with, "Sir, you must be mistaken; there isn't a building at Centennial Park big enough for a circus."

1941 Circus Ad. -Price-

Clover Bottom Beach

By Amelia Whitsitt Edwards

In the 1920s Lebanon Road ran through the Clover Bottom farm property and crossed Stones River just west of the present road and bridge. The old stone bridge abutments are still standing. The Stanford brothers, A.F. and R.D., had purchased the farm in 1918. Since Lebanon Road split the property, A.F. took the section to the east of the road and R.D. took the section to the west. A.F.'s part included the antebellum Hoggatt residence, and R.D. built a two-story brick colonial revival home on his side of the road.

In the period following World War I the outlying areas of Davidson County were still rural farm lands. A.F. Stanford ran a dairy farm at Clover Bottom while R.D. Stanford raised white-faced beef cattle. The majority of the population of the county, however, lived within the confines of the Nashville city limits. With the pro-liferation of the family motor car in the "Roaring Twenties," excursions to the countryside became a popular pastime. For those fortunate enough to own an automobile, exploring country roads, farms, and creek sides was a welcome relief from city life. There was usually a picnic basket on board filled with fried chicken, bis-cuits that had been buttered while hot, stuffed eggs, and a special Nashville favorite, chess pie.

Finding a swimming hole in one of the area rivers or creeks was an extra bonus on these outings. Although Mill Creek and Richland Creek were good for wading, neither furnished very deep holes for swimming. Men and boys swam in the Cumberland River, but it was considered too dangerous for women and children. The best swim-ming spots were found in the Harpeth and Stones rivers.

One such spot on Stones River was on A.F. Stanford's side of the old bridge near where the present-day bridge crosses. Mr. Stan-ford created a beach by having tons of sand hauled in. He constructed a frame beach house with dressing rooms, lockers, and showers. There were boats, springboards, and picnic tables. He even employed Mr. and Mrs. M.B. Hall to manage the beach operation. Mr. Stanford's generosity in creating this community beach is documented in a 1927 advertisement which stated that everything was free. It also stated that Old Hickory busses passed every thirty minutes—fare was twenty-five cents.

When the new bridge was constructed in the early 1930s, the old road leading to the beach entrance was closed. The new bridge piers were sunk into the the swimming hole and floods washed away the sand. All

The Clover Bottom beach house as seen through the Stones River bridge, *circa* 1931. -Davis-

that remains of the once-lively recreational spot are photographs taken by Wiles Studio in 1931, now in the collection of Merle Stanford Davis who married A.F. Stanford in 1927 and was mistress of Clover Bottom until 1948. She has generously shared her photographs and recollections for the publication of this article.

1927 ad for Clover Bottom Beach. -Davis-

Remembering Nashville's Daughters

By Carol Kaplan

March is National Women's History Month, a time to pause and reflect on those who have blazed the trail for us to follow. Here in Nashville it's an easy and informative exercise, for we often hear the names of the women who have lived here and contributed to our city's life. On the other hand, how much do we really know about these ladies, and how many others, just as interesting, have been forgotten?

Caroling for Fannie Battle is a Nashville tradition, but do we know that Miss Fannie, who never received a salary of more than

Fanny Battle gravestone in Mt. Olivet Cemetery.
-Livy Simpson-

$30 a month during her 50 years of service, was sent to prison for spying during the Civil War? Martha O'Bryan, for whom we crank ice cream, found her life's meaning in helping others after her fiancé was executed by the Union Army. Christiana Rains, sliding her toddlers across the frozen Cumberland River to found Nashville on Christmas Day, 1779, and Stella Vaughn, the first woman staff member at Vanderbilt in 1905, are both pioneers.

Slave Sally Thomas saved her money and purchased freedom not for herself but for her little boy. Hetty McEwen flew her Union flag in Confederate Nashville. Mary Kate Patterson brought her friend Sam Davis breakfast on his last Sunday of freedom, galloping her horse so the coffee wouldn't have time to cool.

In antebellum Nashville, teacher Charlotte Fall Fanning was so loved by her pupils that an extra Greek lesson was a sought-after treat. In our own time, Julia Green shocked men drivers by driving her Ford. Miss Julia was such a presence that teachers warned of her arrival by passing a green pencil so that everyone would be prepared. Hattie Cotton and Emma B. Clemons spent their lives serving Nashville's children and were rewarded by having schools named for them. Anne Webber didn't attend Watkins Institute, but left her large estate to help others do so.

Known primarily as founder of the UDC, Caroline Meriwether Goodlett also helped the horses of Nashville by founding the Tennessee Humane Society and placing drinking troughs on every corner. Needlework designer Anne Champe Orr provided employment for women in Appalachian Kentucky, who completed the appliquéd quilts and delicate tablecloths her customers wanted to own, but not to make. Elizabeth Eakin devoted her fortune to the welfare and beautification of her city. Eakin School honors her service as the first female member of the Board of Education in 1917. When her four sons went to serve in World War I, Margaret Winston Caldwell ran their automobile dealership, the only woman dealer in the country. Her sister May Winston Caldwell, saddened by the loss of her son in that war, was the guiding spirit of the Peace or Battle of Nashville Monument. Erected in 1927 to commemorate reconciliation and the sacrifice of young men in war, the monument has recently been restored.

Lula Clay Naff was the manager of the Ryman Auditorium for 50 years, retiring in 1955. Rarely seeing a performance, unfazed by Barrymore, Hepburn, or Helen Hayes, Mrs. Naff always made a profit and never allowed any criticism of the facilities. Mary Dorris, Bettie Donelson, Louise Lindsley, and their friends organized the Ladies' Hermitage Association and saved Jackson's home from destruction. Ella Sheppard and her fellow students became the Fisk Jubilee Singers and rescued their university.

Almost all of these women lived and worked before they had the right to vote. Nashville was the battleground for the ratification of the 19th Amendment. Delia Dortch, J. Frankie Pierce, Warner family members, and countless others worked as hard as they ever had, propelled by the vision of leader Anne Dallas Dudley. "We have a vision of a time when a woman's home will be the whole world, her children all those whose feet are bare, and her sisters all who need a helping hand; a vision of a new knighthood, a new chivalry, when men will not fight for women but for the rights of women." Ironically, neither Anne Dudley's nor Kate Burch Warner's own daughters lived to adulthood to use the right for which their mothers had struggled.

These are just a few of the many women who have had an impact on Nashville. From Rhoda Calvert Barnard, who has a planet for a namesake, to Cornelia Clark Fort, sacrificing her young life for her country, Nashville's daughters have lived with bravery and determination. Time and circumstances have made the challenges of each one different, but they are united in their courage and love for their city and country. We owe them respect and honor and have the obligation to keep their memory alive.

Float in the French Day parade in Nashville, July 14, 1918. Standing are Mrs. Meredith Caldwell (Ellen Thomas), Mrs. Henry Frazier (Milbrey Keith), and Mrs. Joseph Palmer (Ann Madden). The National League for Woman's Service was organized in Washington, D.C., in January of 1917. Eager to aid their country in WWI, its membership comprised more than 5,000 women. Mrs. Jesse Overton (Saidee Williams) was the Tennessee president. Her only son, John, was killed in that war. -NR-

The Rebirth of Germantown

By John Lawrence Connelly, Davidson County Historian

For a great part of the 20th century Nashville residents either ignored or did not know that an area north of Jefferson Street was a prominent neighborhood where many of Nashville's leading citizens once lived. To a large extent this was a German community that began flourishing heartily in the 1840s by blending its German heritage with Irish, Italian, Swiss, and Jewish neighbors, in public schools and sometimes in churches. The Catholic Church of the Assumption, founded in 1859, held many of its services in German as did the German Methodist Church (Barth Memorial), founded in 1854 on North College Street (Second Avenue, North). Many prosperous merchants of the city lived in Germantown, and prominent retail names hung on store signs downtown, including Rust, Zugermann, Zickler, Ratterman, Buddeke, Thuss, Grosholz, Jensen, Jeck, and Wheling. In addition, German names in the community reflected a strong Lutheran population.

In the German community many immigrants worked as butchers, a practice brought over from Europe. They often slaughtered meat in their backyards or nearby lots. Eventually, fewer butchers peddled meat from door to door, since the time came when they could sell meat to local markets or to the Nashville Market House. Many would open their own markets or stalls. Names such as Jacobs, Dieterle, Stier, Warner, Oliver, Neuhoff, Power, Petre, Laitenberger, and White were among those from North Nashville. Meat suppliers from Butchertown developed the Christmas spice round, a Nashville holiday meat to become famous.

By 1915 the changes that would eventually destroy the neighborhood were beginning to take place. Just as the people who live in communities do not stay the same, old neighborhoods also change. As streetcar lines expanded and advancement was made in motor transportation shortly after the turn of the century, there was a definite trend for residents to move away from the "walk-to-town" areas. Moreover, the development of refrigeration led to the phasing out of many small butchering businesses. Large packing houses were formed, and they infringed upon the pleasant residential atmosphere of the neighborhood that had often been advertised in local newspapers as a growing and fashionable community. It was World War I, however, that dealt the final blow to Germantown.

Wilbur F. Creighton, in his book *Building of Nashville*, states: "In 1917 the reservoir was closed to visitors. The paper had been filled with stories of German atrocities, such as the use of poisonous gases and deliberate infection of water supplies." Other exaggerated cases included emotional suggestions by some that other citizens "kill their dachshunds." Many German families, therefore, told their older members to please stop speaking German—even at home.

The little German Barth Memorial Church seems to manifest what happened in Germantown. For many years services were altogether spoken in German, but when World War I struck it was resolved that the church have only English services. Catholics and Lutherans with German backgrounds did likewise. The uniqueness of a small community with ties to the "Fatherland" was over. The neighborhood as it once was would never come back, and constant decline ensued until a handful of urban pioneers decided to attempt to create a new Germantown in the 1970s.

As Germantown experienced a great deal of decay, many houses were torn down and others extensively altered. Nonetheless, studies made by the Metropolitan Historical Commission in the 1970s stated: "A large percentage of structures are still intact, and it can become a viable neighborhood. The quality of architecture is exceptional, and the condition of the structures is, for the most part, quite sound."

Nashville's Germantown Historic District is one of the architecturally heterogeneous neighborhoods in the city. The eight-block area contains a wide variety of styles and types of residences built between the 1840s and 1920s. Because of its historical and architectural significance Germantown was listed in the National Register of Historic Places in August 1979.

For the past twenty years new residents have worked individually and collectively on the restoration of Germantown. The Germantown Association is the neighborhood group where old and new residents come together and plan for the future. A ride to the area today reveals a new community with restored houses, new houses, beautiful flowers and trees, a new supermarket, a new pharmacy, and attractive brick sidewalks. Once again Nashville can take pride in a neighborhood located within a few steps of the Bicentennial Mall, with the best view of the State Capitol. Today, it has come back and has almost unlimited potential for tomorrow.

Octoberfest logo. -Connelly-

Twenty years ago members of the Catholic Church of the Assumption and the Monroe Street United Church (two historic churches that remained) gave Nashville its first Oktoberfest. It has become one of Middle Tennessee's most popular celebrations, held on the second Saturday in October. The Germantown Association has sponsored a Maifest celebration for the past decade and sold out all of its tickets this year. Yes, Germantown is on the map again!

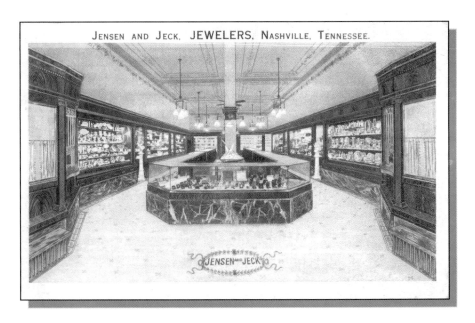

JENSEN AND JECK, JEWELERS, NASHVILLE, TENNESSEE.

Like many other names associated with Germantown, Jensen and Jeck, whose jewelry store is featured in this old postcard, ran a prominent downtown business. *-NHN-*

Nashville School Desegregation

By James Summerville

The 1896 Supreme Court, in *Plessy v. Ferguson*, upheld the constitutionality of social segregation, ruling that state laws which required the separation of the races did not imply the inferiority of either. Yet separate was not equal in Tennessee. A 1930 study of Nashville schools called attention to dilapidated buildings, unsanitary outhouses, and inadequate lighting. Twenty years later, some black students still had to walk a half mile for a drink of water.

On May 17, 1954, the Supreme Court reversed *Plessy*, which had been used by many states to justify public segregation. *Brown v. Board of Education* held that "separate educational facilities" were "inherently unequal" because segregation denied black students equal protection under the law, a violation of the Fourteenth Amendment. A year later, the high court issued its implementation order, directing district federal courts to bring about compliance with the *Brown* decision. This was to be accomplished "with all deliberate speed," an oxymoron which suggested that lower courts could show flexibility.

Nashville's Board of Education appointed a committee to consider its options. There matters would have stayed forever except for the lawsuit filed by Alfred Z. Kelley, an East Nashville barber. Kelley could not see why his son Robert had to commute across town to Pearl High School though the family lived within walking distance of East High School. The simple answer was that East was all white, and the Kelleys were black.

Lawyer Alexander Looby and his partner Avon Williams, Jr., carried *Kelley v. Board of Education* into

Grave marker of Alexander Looby in Greenwood Cemetery. -*NHN*-

federal district court. In time, Judge William E. Miller found for the plaintiff and directed the school board to prepare a plan for desegregation and submit it to the court by January 1957.

The educators stressed "deliberate" rather than "speed" and proposed that a grade a year be integrated, beginning with the first grade that next fall. At the same time, their plan allowed parents of either race to transfer a child out of a school where the other race predominated. Finally, the board redrew the bounds of school zones so that only about 115 black first-graders, out of 1,500 eligible, could enter all-white schools come September.

Despite its novel evasions, the school board had acceded to the *Brown* decision. Diehards were left with unpalatable choices: resistance in public protests or keeping their children out of school.

Some black parents, worried about segregationists' threats, took advantage of the school board's transfer privilege. As a result, the burden of bringing down Jim Crow in public education in Nashville fell on 19 boys and girls. Twelve of them and their parents arrived at six elementary schools on the morning of September 9, 1957. So did knots of jeering white adults and teenagers. Police escorted the youngsters safely inside, but the day passed uneasily.

A few minutes after midnight, a bomb demolished a wing of East Nashville's Hattie Cotton School. The police cracked down on persons carrying weapons, and jailed an agitator, John Kaspar, who had come to town to promote resistance to school desegregation.

The handful of black youngsters who brought down the "walls of Jericho" adapted well, as did their white peers. Ironically, militants like Kaspar led the city to declare itself a peaceful, law-abiding community. Although support for the idea of racial equality was equivocal, the issue was now public order, for which there was universal support. The number of black students in formerly all-white schools grew from a few in 1957 to more than 700 by 1963. This was hardly a social revolution, but it did preface the gradual acceptance by Nashville parents, black and white, that the old days of separate and unequal schools were finished.

Civil Rights and the Nashville Room

By Sue Loper

Four decades ago, during a time of sweeping social change throughout our nation, a determined group of Nashville students began a nonviolent revolution in this city that changed history. On February 13, 1960, after months of workshops centered on the methods of nonviolent protest, a group of African-American students from local universities sat down at a lunch counter and refused to move until they were served.

This was the start of the sit-in movement in Nashville, inaugurating what Martin Luther King, Jr., deemed the best-organized movement in the South. It was not an easy process; response to the group's activities was sometimes violent. Nevertheless, the movement grew, as individuals and groups raised bail money or represented the students in court. One of those advocates was lawyer Z. Alexander Looby. Because of his support of the protestors, Looby's home was bombed on April 19, 1960. Later that day the students led a spontaneous march on the courthouse to confront Nashville's mayor. Diane Nash, spokesperson for the group, asked Mayor Ben West whether he thought it morally right for a restaurant to deny an individual a meal because of the color of his skin. Mayor West agreed the practice was wrong.

That moment sparked important changes in the city but was not the end of the student movement. Many went on to join the Freedom Riders and to work faithfully in voter registration efforts all over the South.

Years later David Halberstam described the experiences of those students in his book *The Children*. Nashvillian Bill King was so moved by the author's description of the fortitude, persistence, and faith of the young protestors, he believed the events in Nashville and the work of "the children" should be memorialized.

In 2001 Mr. King and his wife Robin, friends of the Nashville Public Library, set up an endowment enabling the library to create a civil rights collection focusing on the Nashville sit-in movement. The collection includes print materials, an oral history project, an

Bill King, John Lewis (D-GA), and Robin King, 02-15-04. -GL-

audio-visual library, microfilm research materials, and a collection of dissertations.

A library space was redesigned to intensify the focus of the collection. The new area opened on December 6, 2003, and is now a mainstay of the Nashville Public Library Special Collections Division, The Nashville Room. The setting includes a symbolic lunch counter and stools: glass "placemats" on the countertop list the ten rules sit-in participants were required to follow, and a timeline of national, state, and local civil rights events adorns the backsplash of the

Open House at the Civil Rights Room, 12-06-03. -GL-

counter. Large photographs around the room depict highlights of the movement. A media room and a classroom/lecture space offer screens and touchpads for individual and group viewing. On a glass wall are the words of Martin Luther King, Jr.: "I come to Nashville not to bring inspiration, but to gain inspiration from the great movement that has taken place in this community." Over the doorway is a quote by John Lewis, one of the 1961 students, now a U. S. Representative from Georgia: "If not us, then who; if not now, then when?"

At the dedication of the room, February 14-15, 2004, John Lewis, moved to tears upon seeing his quotation over the doorway, stood in the civil rights room as the leader of the "Faith and Politics Tour," which travels annually, with invited U.S. legislators, to significant civil rights locations. Lewis's co-chair for this trip was Senate Majority Leader Bill Frist. The library's Saturday civil rights workshops drew 800 people; 1300 came to hear the panel speak on Sunday. This powerful discussion, moderated by John Seigenthaler, featured Reverend C. T. Vivian, Reverend James Lawson, Diane Nash, Congressman John Lewis (Georgia), Reverend James Bevel, and Reverend Bernard Lafayette, speaking to the overflow crowd. Other program participants included Nashville Library Director Donna Nicely, Nashville Mayor Bill Purcell and Vice-Mayor Howard Gentry, U.S. Congressman Jim Cooper and Senator Bill Frist, and Tennessee Governor Phil Bredesen. The program concluded with the singing of "We Shall Overcome," led by Guy and Candie Carawan, folk singers whose songs have long inspired the civil rights movement. No one wanted the program to end: the library, scheduled to close at 5:00, remained open until after 7:00.

The program and reception were funded in part by the First Baptist Church Capitol Hill, a gathering place for sixties protestors and a training site for nonviolent protest activity. Other supporters included The First Amendment Center and The William Winter Center for Racial Justice, with primary support for the event coming from Robin and Bill King.

Additional contributions included a photographic exhibit of the civil rights movement by Harold Lowe; a film provided by Nashville Public Television, from their production entitled *Nashville Memories*; and a film of the event made by Metro Channel 3, which continues to make it available. Nashville Public Television filmed segments of the program for their popular series, *Tennessee Cross-roads*.

Today the civil rights room is an active place. Cumberland Valley Girl Scouts use its resources as they work on civil rights badges. Schools, churches, and civic groups come for tours; colleges and universities use the Lowe Photograph Collection. Staff members are working with Fisk University to prepare a traveling exhibit about the women of the civil rights movement. The Civil Rights Oral History Collection continues to grow as the words of participants are captured for future generations. Recently a correspondent from the Azerbaijani newspaper *Baku Sun* asked to copy the photograph of the silent march to the courthouse. The photograph will accompany the *Sun's* interview with USAID Country Coordinator William McKinney, who was a participant in the Nashville sit-ins. The seeds planted by Nashville's nonviolent revolution continue to produce fruit.

Singing "We Shall Overcome" at the dedication of the Civil Rights Room are, L to R, Rev. C.T. Vivian, John Seigenthaler, Rev. James Lawson, Diane Nash, John Lewis (D-GA), Dr. James Bevel, and Dr. Bernard Lafayette. 02-15-04.
-GL-

TSLA--Tennessee's Treasurehouse

By Kathy Lauder

In early January 2004 Herbert Harper of the Tennessee Historical Commission announced that the Tennessee State Library and Archives (TSLA) "has, upon the nomination of this office, been placed in the National and Tennessee Registers of Historic Places by the National Park Service of the United States Department of the Interior on November 17, 2003."

TSLA was declared eligible for the National Register on two counts. The first is architecture. Designed by H. Clinton Parrent, Jr., and completed in 1953, the structure is considered an outstanding example of late neoclassical architecture. Introduced at the 1893 World's Columbian Exposition in Chicago, the neoclassical style is marked by "a symmetrical façade featuring a central entrance shielded by a full-height porch with a roof supported by classical columns." TSLA features the slender columns and side-gabled roofs of the later phase, along with some Art Deco touches. It was designed to complement, although not to duplicate, the neighboring Capitol and Supreme Court buildings.

The September 1953 edition of the *Tennessee Historical Quarterly*, reporting on the grand opening of the building, included this enthusiastic description: "With its exterior walls of white Tennessee marble, its Roman Ionic columns suggestive of the Greek Ionic columns of the Capitol and the inscriptions along the upper walls which serve as reminders of the cultural traditions out of which the building grew, it adds immeasurably to the beauty of Capitol Hill. The building is as functional as it is beautiful, with eight stack levels to accommodate [two million volumes of] books and records . . ., a restoration laboratory for the repair and preservation of old books and records, a photographic laboratory . . ., and an auditorium."

One of the most surprising features of TSLA is that it is, in fact, two very different buildings under one roof. The handsome front section, containing the public reading rooms and staff offices, consists of three stories and an attic storage area. A highlight is the elegant marble vestibule, featuring a terrazzo floor embellished with a geographical map of Tennessee, and military symbols reminding visitors that the building is dedicated to the Tennessee veterans of World War II. The rear of the building, functional and much less ornate, consists of eight stories of stacks and work areas.

Return Jonathan Meigs
-TSLA-

The original State Library was housed in the Capitol. Architect William Strickland himself designed the lofty and elegant room across from the Supreme Court chambers. In 1854 the legislature appropriated funds to purchase books, appointing Return Jonathan Meigs to build the collection. Meigs, a respected scholar, was named first State Librarian in 1856. By the middle of the 20th century, his successors had overseen many changes in the library, including the acquisition of the Tennessee Historical Society papers in 1927. As the collection grew, particularly under the leadership of John Trotwood Moore, who developed the collection of military and other historical records, the allotted space became cramped. It became clear that the Capitol-based Library was no longer an effective facility for research and study.

For that reason, the educational value of the current facility--its second criterion of eligibility for the National Register--may be even more significant. The building was constructed not only to store the State Library's growing collection, but also to preserve the state's archival records after many decades in which they were stuffed into attics, cellars, and odd corners of the Capitol and other buildings. In the early 1890s a janitor had actually burned several cartloads of documents, saying they were "wet and nasty and smelled bad." An 1893 request to ship 85 trunks of Civil War vouchers to Washington, D.C., led Governor Peter Turney to assign Capitol superintendent Robert Thomas Quarles to find them. Quarles became the hero of Tennessee historians forever when he focused attention on the appalling condition of stored records and began a ten-year effort to sort and preserve them. After Quarles's death in 1914, the state legislature passed a resolution authorizing the governor to appoint a state official to continue the work of sorting and preserving. John Trotwood Moore was named the first State Librarian and Archivist in 1919, and the Library and Archives officially merged in 1921.

Construction of the current building was proposed at the first meeting of the Tennessee Historical Commission on December 3, 1941, by Moore's widow and successor, Mary Daniel Moore. Unfortunately, the entry of the United States into World War II four days later forced the plans to be delayed for several years. Finally, in 1947 and 1949, under the administrations of Governors Jim McCord and Gordon Browning, the state legislature appropri-

TSLA under construction. -TSLA-

ated the necessary funds to begin construction. Ground was broken in 1951; the formal opening took place on June 17, 1953.

The author is grateful to Dr. Edwin Gleaves, Jeanne Sugg, Fran Schell, Greg Poole, and Ralph Sowell, who graciously shared the documents and information used in the preparation of this essay.

TSLA from the southeast, 2004. -Lauder-

The Metropolitan Nashville-Davidson County Government Archives: Twenty-three Years and Counting

By Kenneth Fieth, Metropolitan Nashville Archivist

...we first took the matter of building vaults into considera-tion and found the court house so awkwardly constructed that the building of vaults would greatly obstruct the light and diminish the space to such an extent as to make this method impractible [sic] *and it would cost a very large amount, more than we could recommend to be expended on this diliapated* [sic] *and ill constructed building.*

With that, a committee appointed to "report on what was to be done to preserve the county papers and records" went on to recommend "Wolfi patent roller shelving" and file "cases" to preserve the records of the county in the antebellum Davidson County court-house. The committee suggested this would be a money-saving venture since the shelving and file cabinets could be moved into a new courthouse "which at no distant day we hope to see."

That was 1897. It would be another 39 years before the vener-able old courthouse, whose walls bore witness to the days of secession, war, and recovery, was destroyed to make way for a new structure, completed in 1937. Apparently, the shelving and file cases also fell to the journeyman's hammer.

It would be another 44 years before the question of what to do with over 200 years of history was again contemplated. In 1980 Mayor Richard Fulton saw the need to create an archives for the preservation of the historical records of the city and county. The mayor established an archives advisory committee, and work began thereafter to establish an archives for Davidson County.

Mayor Fulton determined that an archives facility should be placed under the Nashville Public Library. In discussions with Pub-lic Library Director Marshall Stewart, Mrs. Virginia Lyle, a member of the Nashville Public Library board, was asked to be the first Metropolitan Archivist.

Archives facilities on Elm
Hill Pike. *-NHN-*

From 1981 to 1985 the Archives consisted of a room in the Stahlman building. In March of 1985 the Metro Council appropriated $150,000 for the renovation of the former Mt. Zeno school, a Metro-owned building on Elm Hill Pike, as the Metro Archives.

Opening in August of 1986, the Metropolitan Archives held some three million records dating from the 1800s to the late 20th century. A second building was planned and work began in 1987. In 1988 severe budget reductions within Metropolitan Government halted construction on the nearly completed adjacent building and called for the closure of the Archives as well as the return of thousands of records to the originating departments.

With pressure from Nashville citizens and historical associations, the Archives remained open, with very limited operating hours and a single staff member throughout 1988-1989. Funding gradually increased, and by 1993 the Metro Archives improved to three staff members and 40 operating hours per week.

In 1994 the Archives began active discussions with the Metro departments that maintained historical records. Working with these departments as well as the Davidson County court system (whose enormous volume of historical records provided some interesting challenges for space allocation), the Archives grew to over five million records dating from the 1780s.

In 2000 the new Green Hills Branch Library was completed, and the old branch building became available for the Archives. Currently the public reference services of the Archives are located in the old building at 3801 Green Hills Village Drive, and records not highly active for research are stored in the Elm Hill Pike building.

In addition to photographic services and digitization of historical records, the Archives offers quarterly exhibits highlighting the history of Nashville and Davidson County. The most recent exhibit, "Play Ball: A Look at Nashville Baseball," included a panel discussion featuring some of the last players from the Nashville Vols and Negro League. The discussion, filmed by Metro Channel 3 and covered by local sports, radio, and television broadcasts, is a testimony to the value of interaction between the community and the local archives.

In 2004 the Metropolitan Government Archives has two buildings, six employees plus volunteers, programs in microfilming and conservation, and a Friends of the Archives group. The two facilities hold over five million

Pictured are Joe Stupak, pitcher for the Nashville Vols in 1954, and Metro Archives employees Linda Center and Kenneth Fieth. 9-19-04. *-NHN-*

records and several thousand volumes. The collection includes 50,000 photographs, 60,000 feet of motion picture film, and thousands of feet of audio and video recordings. These represent the collective memory of our city, establishing our identity and linking us to a long and eventful past.

The Archives facility in Green Hills. -Fieth-

The Archives' visitors--about 9,000 per year--have come from as near as Hillsboro High School and as far as Sophia, Bulgaria, to gain an understanding of the history of Nashville and how that history is preserved. The Metropolitan Government Archives operating hours are Monday-Friday, 9:30 a.m.-5:30 p.m.

Reminiscence

My Hermitage Experience

By Houston Seat

My first visit to The Hermitage, at the age of five years, was with my grandfather in a borrowed Model A Ford. I had to remain in the car and be good, and I didn't get to go into this big brick house even though I really wanted to see what was inside. Perhaps I should explain.

My grandfather, Samuel H. Seat, was a blacksmith adept at working with iron and fashioning hand-wrought objects. The quality of his work was well known, and he was often occupied in some special project. It was 1935 at the time, and the Ladies' Hermitage Association contacted my grandfather about reproducing the latch assembly on the window shutters of the mansion since time had taken toll on the original iron pieces. I had to remain in the Ford while he was inside meeting with the ladies in charge of the restoration. Memory brings back the wasp that came through the open car window buzzing me for a few moments and then flying on toward the big house with the loose, sagging shutters.

As time passed I learned that this was the home of Andrew Jackson and his wife, Rachel, who died suddenly on December 22, 1828, the year Andrew was elected President of our country. Rachel is quoted as saying, "I had rather be a doorkeeper in the house of God than to live in that palace at Washington." Was her wish granted?

On a return visit thirty years later, I had a five-year-old with me—my son. We toured The Hermitage together. The Model A Ford is past history, as is the grandparent who let me tag along. Memories can last a lifetime, and those with whom we experience special occasions live on, too.

Document

Below is a rare Nashville newspaper article from The Clarion, & Tennessee State Gazette, *published Tuesday, March 15, 1814.*

Submitted by Larry Michael Ellis

Dreadful Fire ! ! !

Under the dispensations of divine providence, we have again to record the destructive effects of of [*sic*] this ungovernable element. - On Friday night last, about 10 o'clock, the citizens of this town were alarmed with the cry of fire! It proceeded from the hay-loft of Wm. W. Cooke, Esq. near Mr. Woods [*sic*] warehouse; it had gained such an ascendency [*sic*] & the buildings were so combustible, that the utmost exertions of the citizens could not save the large adjoining warehouse, filled with consignments to Joseph Woods esq commission merchant, the bindery, dwelling house and bookstore of Mr. Duncan Robertson, the tavern house of Robert Renfroe, the frame house of John Anderson esq, the house occupied by Mr. Ernest Benoit, baker, the shop of Messrs. E. and G. Hewlett saddlers above; the dwelling house of Wm. W. Cooke esq, the dwelling house occupied by Mr. S. V. Stout, the warehouse of Messrs. Read and Washington, army contractors, and their office, the shop & dwelling house of Mr. D. C. Snow, tin plate worker, below; the dwelling house of Joseph T. Elliston, and his silversmith shop, the dwelling house of the editor of the Clarion, & his printing office, the house lately occupied by Wm. M. Wallace, as a shoemaker's shop and the house occupied be Joseph Sumner, the property of Mr. John Young, the office of the Nashville Whig, and the hatter's shop of Mr. Joshua Pilcher, and the brick store-house occupied by W. Tannehill, esq. above on the east of Market street, & all the frame buildings on the same side opposite to bank alley, making in the whole the most destructive fire ever experienced in the western country. No language can paint the distress of many of the sufferers, who were left without bread, meat, dishes or plates, or a covering except the heavens. In the whole range of the fire we are however gratified that no lives were lost, and we hope that in a few years a majority of the sufferers will be able to replace the property they have thus lost.

In some few cases we are, however, sorry to learn the individuals are ruined. It is impossible at present to form any estimate of the immense loss sustained - nearly one half the buildings that were in the town are in ashes; much furniture and other valuable property was lost in the flames. Among the sufferers, the Editor of this Paper finds it necessary to repeat that he was one - his Printing Office contained many printed books and pamphlets, the most of which were lost, and he is sorry to state, in that situation is the Journal of the proceedings of the last Gener- Assembly [*sic*], which was nearly entirely lost. Of the Journal of the house of Representatives, it is believed a copy can be made out; but of the Senate, there is not the least hope of ever recovering one, for the printing and manuscript shared the same fate. Of the heavy editions of law books, &c. &c in the house, it is believed scarcely a copy remains; and of the printing apparatus, a considerable part was lost; but one press and nearly all the type was saved. For the satisfaction of the members of the last General Assembly, he is thus particular, that the loss of the public Journals may be rightly understood.

The fire was communicated, we have little doubt, by some incendiary - who is not yet ascertained.

> *"Much history, and therefore much of the stream of life, passes us by— never recorded, never honored, and after a while, never remembered."*
> *-NHN-*

The Contributors to this Volume

Mike Slate (p. 7) is the founder and publisher of the *Nashville Historical Newsletter.* A Nashville native, he attended Metro public schools and holds degrees from David Lipscomb College, George Peabody College, and Harding Graduate School (Memphis). His greatest "accomplishment" is his son, Timothy Slate. Mike is married to *NHN* editor Kathy Lauder, from whom he has almost learned where to place commas.

Doris Boyce (p. 9), the mother of five and grandmother of eleven, is a Nashvillian who has been self-employed in the custom window treatment business since 1987. She considers herself a story-teller rather than a historian. As a member of a writers group that meets twice a month, Doris has written numerous poems, short stories, children's stories, folk tales, and non-fiction. She has two books in manuscript, an adult history and a young-adult novel. Her work has been published in *Sisters in Crime*, *International Poets*, the *1997 Williamson County Literary Review*, and the *Nashville Historical Newsletter*.

Bonnie Ross Meador (p. 11) received her degree in English from Aurora College (Illinois) in 1974. For more than 23 years she has worked as designer, compositor, and journalist at *The Citizen-Times*, a 114-year-old weekly newspaper in Scottsville, Kentucky. Married for 32 years, Bonnie has two children and four grandchildren. In addition to genealogy and history, she enjoys swimming at her local YMCA, where she is a lifeguard and aquatics instructor.

Deborah Oeser Cox (p. 14) is a native of Northeast Nashville and a 9th generation Nashvillian. She has been employed by the Metropolitan Government Archives, located in Green Hills, since 1997. Debie's interest in and research into the early history of Nashville began as a young teen after reading Alfred Leland Crabb's *Journey to Nashville*. She was married in 1969 to Jimmy Cox. Debie and Jimmy have two daughters, Tammy Miller and Amanda Cox, and two grandchildren, Layton and Lauren Miller.

Susan Douglas Wilson (p. 18) is a 7th generation Nashvillian. She graduated from McGavock High School and earned B.S. and M.S. degrees from George Peabody College for Teachers. Her early love of history originated from stories of Nashville life told to her by her father and his family. Susan has written articles for scientific, educational, and genealogical publications. She currently lives in Brentwood, Tennessee, with her husband, Rick.

Guy Alan Bockmon (p. 21), author of *Madison Station*, was born December 7, 1926, at Paducah, KY. Music was his primary interest throughout his academic years at Tilghman High School, Murray State University, and the Eastman School of Music. He was a professor of music at the University of Tennessee for 18 years before moving to Nashville to start a branch at UT Nashville. His writing career began at Knoxville when he co-authored and edited music textbooks. Since retirement he has time to enjoy his lifetime interest in history.

Linda Center (p. 23) has been a staff member of the Metropolitan Government Archives since 1995. She came to the Archives from the Metro Historical Commission where she completed an architectural survey of Davidson County. The survey included more than 25,000 structures over 50 years old. Center holds a B.A. degree in English and completed course work towards a master's degree in Historic Preservation at MTSU. A native of Rutherford County, she and her husband John have lived in Nashville since 1976. Their son and his family live in Murfreesboro.

Ilene Jones Cornwell (p. 27), author and editor, has been a leader in Tennessee cultural, historical, and environmental issues since 1968. Her efforts on behalf of Natchez Trace preservation have received national recognition. She is well known for her research and writings on local and state history, as well as on women's history, particularly woman suffrage. Her honors and awards include listings in *Who's Who in America*, *Who's Who of American Women*, and *2,000 Notable American Women*. Ilene is founder of the Tennessee Women's Network and executive director of the West Nashville Founders' Museum, Inc., sponsor of the James Robertson Log House replica in H.G. Hill Park.

Dave Price (p. 34) denies that he came to Nashborough as an infant with the Donelson party; however, he remembers when the Jere Baxter School burned, and he can recall boarding streetcars in the Transfer Station. He saw stage shows at the original Princess Theater (the one across Church Street from Lebeck's), and he was in the present Ben West Traffic Court Building when it was the Market House. Dave grew up seeing circuses at Centennial Park and later at the Fair Grounds, and he eventually spent nine years on the road as an advance man for some of the last of the big tent shows.

Amelia Whitsitt Edwards (p. 37), who grew up in historic Edgefield, has lived in Donelson since her marriage in 1951. She is currently vice-chairman of the Metropolitan Historical Commission. The author of the books *Nashville Interiors 1866 to 1920* and *Growing Up in Edgefield*, Edwards donated the proceeds from both books to historical causes. She has written for various historical publications and has produced a number of unpublished historical manuscripts.

Carol Farrar Kaplan (p. 39) is a 7th generation Nashvillian. A graduate of George Peabody College, she has been on the staff of the Nashville Room of the Public Library for more than twenty years. Kaplan is a former board member of Historic Nashville, Inc. and the City Cemetery Association. She is co-author of *Remember the Ladies: Women of Mt. Olivet Cemetery* (with Livy Simpson) and *The Nashville City Cemetery: History Carved in Stone* (with Carole Bucy).

John Lawrence Connelly (p. 42), Nashville writer of local history, is a retired entrepreneur and educator. He is former chairman of the Metropolitan Historical Commission and appointed member for the past 25 years. Connelly is the "founding father" of Germantown's Oktoberfest celebration, as well as founder of Friends of the Metro Archives. In 1996 the Metropolitan Council named him official historian of Davidson County. He has received numerous awards for

accomplishments. Currently, he writes a column, "Historically Speaking," for *The News*, published by Gary Cunningham.

James Summerville (p. 45), a Nashville native, lives in the historic Hillsboro-West End neighborhood. He received his B.A. from the University of Tennessee and earned master's degrees from Iowa and Vanderbilt universities. The author of many respected historical books and articles, he is considered the driving force behind the restoration and relocation of the Battle of Nashville Monument. Summerville is a recipient of the Moore Memorial Award for Best Published Article of the Year in Tennessee History.

Dr. Sue Loper (p. 47) is the Manager of the Special Collections Division (including the Nashville Room) of the Nashville Public Library. Early in her career she worked in Charlotte, NC, and St. Louis, MO, as a teacher in social studies and English. After graduating from George Peabody College with a Master of Library Science degree, she held library positions in Mississippi and Tennessee, including Director of the Finney Memorial Library and Learning Resources Center at Columbia State Community College. Loper received her doctorate in Administrative Leadership from Vanderbilt University in 1988.

Kathy Lauder (p. 51), editor of the *Nashville Historical Newsletter*, works at the Tennessee State Library and Archives. She lived in nine states and traveled widely in North America and Europe before settling in Nashville. Lauder taught high school English for 30 years, specializing in grammar and composition, world literature, poetry, and dramatic arts. Many of her acting students now work in professional theatre, and a play under her direction took first place in the Maine Drama Festival in 2003. She is the mother of two sons and the grandmother of the wonder-twins, Nicholas and George Gamble.

Kenneth Fieth (p. 54) is the Metropolitan Archivist for Nashville and Davidson County. He received his M.A. degree in historic preservation from MTSU in 1982. He began his archival career with the Tennessee State Library and Archives in 1983 and became the Metro Nashville Archivist in 1993. In 1989 he became a member of the American Academy of Certified Archivists.

Houston Seat (p. 57) grew up in Donelson, Tennessee, and graduated from David Lipscomb College. After two years of military service, he settled in the Nashville area, where his work for the local International Harvester dealership was followed by ten years of self-employment. Seat now works for the Tennessee Department of Human Services. He is a charter member of the Friends of the Metro Archives and has served as its treasurer for ten years.

Larry Michael Ellis (p. 58) is the author of the historical novel *SPIZZERINCTUM: The Life and Legend of Robert "Black Bob" Renfro*. A 6th generation Tennessean, he was born and raised in Clarksville. He served in the United States Navy from 1957-1961 and graduated from Austin Peay State University (B.S., 1965) and MTSU (M.P.A., 1971). Ellis was the Director of the Tennessee Governor's Highway Safety Program for almost 20 years, serving four different governors.

Index

> ## "We did not just happen upon the present: the past is the impetus for today."
> ### -NHN-